Prehistoric Monsters
Did the Strangest Things

First paperback edition, 1990
Abridged edition

Library of Congress Cataloging-in-Publication Data:
Hornblow, Leonora. Prehistoric monsters did the strangest things / written by Leonora and Arthur Hornblow ; illustrated by Sy Barlowe. p. cm.—(Step-up nature books) SUMMARY: Briefly describes, in chronological order, many of the strange animals that lived on earth between the time life began and the appearance of humans. ISBN: 0-394-84307-X (pbk.); 0-394-94307-4 (lib. bdg.) 1. Vertebrates, Fossil—Juvenile literature. [1. Prehistoric animals. 2. Fossils] I. Hornblow, Arthur. II. Barlowe, Sy, ill. III. Title. IV. Series. QE842.H67 1989 566—dc19 88-30212

Manufactured in the United States of America 1 2 3 4 5 6 7 8 9 0

Prehistoric Monsters
Did the Strangest Things

By Leonora and Arthur Hornblow
Illustrated by Sy Barlowe

Abridged Edition

STEP-UP BOOKS

Random House New York

CONTENTS

1

THE BALL OF FIRE

Billions and billions of years ago there were no people. There were no animals. There were no trees or flowers. Our earth was made of gases and stardust. It was a huge ball of fire. No one is sure how this fire began. But it burned all the time.

The earth kept on burning inside. But after billions of years the outside began to cool off. It started to crack. Boiling mud and hot rock gushed out. Clouds of steam hung over the earth. The clouds turned to rain. Water was everywhere. Now life on the earth could begin.

2

THE WET ONES

Life began in the water. The water then was warm and salty. The air was hot and damp. Little plants began to grow. Soon small creatures started to crawl on the bottom of the sea.

After a long time, some of these strange crawlers turned into fish. At first they were very small. Over many, many years some kinds of fish grew larger and larger.

Some fish became sharks. There are still sharks in the sea today. Some sharks now are bigger than those sharks of millions of years ago. Some are smaller. But they are all still the same in many ways. Their bodies are covered with thousands of scales. These are like tiny teeth. Their mouths are filled with real teeth. They are fierce and hungry fish. That is the way sharks have always been. It is strange that they have changed so little—and the world has changed so much.

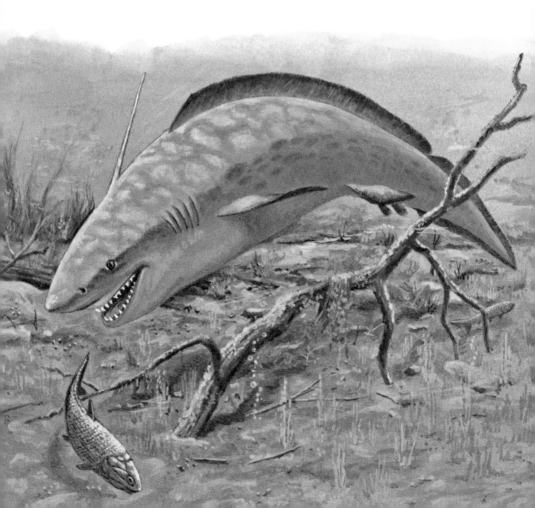

3
LAND HO!

For millions of years, every creature lived in the sea. Slowly, as time went on, rocks and sand rose out of the water. Some sea creatures crawled up on this land. One of the early crawlers was the strange-looking Diplocaulus (dip-luh-CALL-us). He had such an odd head. It looked like an arrow! But Diplocaulus couldn't stay

long on land. His legs were small and very weak. He could not crawl far. He had to go back into the water to find food and to keep his skin wet.

Seymouria (see-MOR-ee-uh) spent most of his time on land. He was a small creature. His legs were strong, so he was able to crawl far from the sea. He looked for plants and insects to eat. The air was cooler than it had been, and more plants were growing. Many insects were living among the plants. So little Seymouria could choose a tasty dinner.

4

SUNNY-SIDE OUT

Dimetrodon (die-MEH-truh-don) lived on land all the time. He was a reptile. There are still reptiles on earth. But nothing like Dimetrodon!

Dimetrodon had lots of teeth. Some teeth were large and some were small. But they were all sharp. Dimetrodon needed them because he did not eat plants. This reptile ate other reptiles.

The strangest thing about Dimetrodon was the piece of skin on his back. It looked like a sail. But he did not use it as a sail. It did not help him move faster.

He probably used his "sail" to help keep him warm. When he felt cold, he would turn sideways. Then his sail would soak up the sun's heat. Lucky Dimetrodon. He had his own built-in heater.

5

THE MAGIC EYES

Some reptiles lived in the water all the time. Ichthyosaurus (ICK-thee-uh-SOR-us) was one of these. He looked like a big fish, but he was really a reptile. He ate other sea creatures. He dove down deep to hunt for food. Ichthyosaurus was a fierce hunter. He had long jaws and as many as 200 sharp teeth.

Around his eyes Ichthyosaurus had

rings of bone. These bony rings could become larger or smaller. This may have helped him see better in the dark water. And when he dove, the rings got smaller. This kept the water from pressing against his eyes. A strange trick to us, but an easy one for Ichthyosaurus.

6

WHAT MARY FOUND

Only a little more than a hundred years ago, an English girl named Mary Anning was looking for seashells. She found the bones of an Ichthyosaurus! Scientists were very excited—all the ichthyosaurs had been dead for millions of years. Since Mary, many people in many places have dug up the bones of other prehistoric animals. Putting the bones together is like doing a jigsaw puzzle. And people have found animal footprints and outlines of plants from millions of years ago. Over the years these had turned to stone. These

bones and outlines are called fossils.

Fossils are very important. They help us learn about the earliest animals. These animals lived millions of years before there were any people. There was no one to write about them. There was no one to draw their pictures. Fossils are the only way we know about these prehistoric monsters. There are fossils and bones in many museums. If you visit them, remember Mary Anning . . . and what she found.

7

HERE COME THE DINOSAURS

In prehistoric times the land was almost always changing. Great mountains rose where there were no mountains before. And there were new lakes and deserts. The air was hot and dry. The reptiles liked this heat. They grew bigger and stronger. It was a good time for reptiles.

A new kind of reptile was roaming the earth—the dinosaur (DIE-nuh-sor). *Dinosaur* means "terrible reptile." Many dinosaurs were terrible; all dinosaurs seem strange to us now. For millions of years they were the rulers of the world.

We always think of dinosaurs as big creatures. But one of the first dinosaurs was small. He was Compsognathus (COMP-sog-NAH-thus). He was the size of a rabbit, but he was a mighty fighter. His front legs were like claws. He walked upright as people do. That made it easier for him to run after his prey. And he could run fast. When he caught a victim, he held him tight in his claws. Then he ate him. After his feast he crouched down and rested. And he watched for another victim to pass by.

8

GIANTS

One of the biggest dinosaurs was Apatosaurus (AH-pat-uh-SOR-us). He had a tiny brain, but he was almost 80 feet long. He weighed about 60,000 pounds. When he walked, his footsteps might have sounded like thunder. He used to be called Brontosaurus (BRONT-uh-SOR-us). *Brontosaurus* means "thunder reptile."

Apatosaurus was a land animal. He spent most of his time eating plants. His long neck helped him to reach the leaves on the tallest trees. It took a lot of plants to fill Apatosaurus's huge stomach.

But there were even bigger dinosaurs. One of them was Brachiosaurus (BRAKE-ee-uh-SOR-us). Like Apatosaurus, he was a plant eater. But his neck was a lot longer, and he was a lot taller. He was tall enough to peer over the top of a four-story building!

Many dinosaurs had short, weak front legs. Brachiosaurus had long, strong front legs. And Brachiosaurus had his nose in a very strange place. It was in a bump on the top of his head. His eyes were just below the bump. No one knows why!

9

THE TERRIBLE TAIL

Stegosaurus (STEG-uh-SOR-us) was a dinosaur whose name means "roofed reptile." The name is perfect for Stegosaurus, because he was very well covered. He had large, bony plates on his back and tail. At the end of his tail there were four sharp spikes.

Stegosaurus had a very tiny brain. It

was so small that it needed help. So Stegosaurus had a kind of second brain where his tail began. This "second brain" controlled his tail. When he was in danger, he would lash out with his spiked tail. When he was left alone, Stegosaurus was peaceful. He ate plants. Most of the time the meat-eating dinosaurs probably left him alone. Maybe they were afraid of the terrible tail with a "mind" of its own.

10

UP AND AWAY

There were reptiles on land. There were reptiles in the sea. And now there were reptiles in the air. One of these was Rhamphorhynchus (RAM-fuh-RINK-us). He had a piece of skin that stretched from his front legs to his back claws. He could flap this skin to fly. He could also glide and float in the air like a little kite. At the tip of his long tail he had another flap of skin. It helped him to steer. The reptile that got off the ground must have been a strange sight.

About the time Rhamphorhynchus was flapping and gliding, another strange

creature was also flying. He was
Archaeopteryx (AR-kee-OP-ter-icks). He
had the beak and feathers of a bird, but
the teeth of a reptile. He could not stay
up in the air very long. Luckily for him,
he had claws on his wings. When he
wanted to rest, he could grab on to a rock
or a tree. He never flew very far. But the
odd Archaeopteryx was our world's first
flyer with feathers. He was the first
known bird.

11

THE FRILLY MONSTER

The world was still changing. The air was cooler. More trees and more plants were growing. And there were flowers now. This was the time of some of the strangest dinosaurs of all.

One of them was Styracosaurus (sty-RAK-uh-SOR-us). He had huge horns on his head. They made him look fierce. But he used them only to defend himself. If he was left alone, he was a peaceful dinosaur. He did not have to kill animals for food. He ate only plants. His teeth worked like scissors. They cut the plants.

If one tooth fell out, he always had another one growing under it. Styracosaurus could keep right on eating.

Around his neck Styracosaurus had a bony frill. It was made of six sharp spikes. That made it hard for an enemy to bite the back of his neck. Styracosaurus was born with this frill. It grew as he did. And he grew to be very heavy. He was too heavy to walk upright as many dinosaurs did. The frilly monster just clumped along on his four thick legs.

12

THE ODD-BILLS

Imagine a dinosaur with a bill like a duck! That sounds strange, but there were many kinds of duck-billed dinosaurs. They lived on land and ate plants.

Many duckbills had odd crests of bone on top of their heads. Some crests were shaped like feathers. Some looked like helmets; others like dinner plates or axe blades. These crests might have helped different kinds of duckbills to recognize each other.

13

THE SNAP
AND THE GULP

Elasmosaurus (ee-LAZ-muh-SOR-us) was a
reptile who spent all his time in the sea.
He was a very long creature. And he had
strong paddle legs. Every day he rowed
himself through the water with his legs.

He could even row backward! He looked for fish to eat. When he saw a fish, out went his long neck. His strong jaws took hold of the fish. Snap! His mouth closed over it. And that was the end of the fish.

The giant lizard Tylosaurus (TIE-luh-SOR-us) also lived in the sea and hunted for fish. He had paddles like Elasmosaurus, but he used his long tail to swim. His powerful tail swished through the water from side to side. Tylosaurus looked fierce, and he was fierce. His jaws were strong and full of sharp teeth. And he could open his mouth very, very wide. Tylosaurus could eat a whole fish in one great gulp.

14

THE SWIMMING HOUSE

The first turtles lived on land. So did many of their later relatives. But after millions of years some turtles moved into the sea. Each new family of turtles grew bigger and bigger. At last the biggest turtle of all appeared. This was Archelon (ARK-uh-lon). He looked like a turtle we might meet now, except for his great size. Archelon was as big as a car!

This giant lived to be more than a hundred years old. Turtles of today also live for many years. One reason is that

they can live for some time without food. Another reason is that they carry their own shelters—the shells on their backs. These shell "houses" keep them safe from their enemies. And no turtle is ever very far from home.

15

THE SKY DIVER

Pteranodon (ter-AN-uh-don) lived millions of years after Rhamphorhynchus. He was a flyer too. But he could fly much farther. His wide wings could carry him far out over the sea. There he would hunt for food. He liked to eat fish. When he saw one, he would dive down. He would catch the fish with his sharp beak. He was very quick. He may even have taken fish away from the fierce sea reptiles.

16

GOOD-BYE, DINOSAURS

The last and largest of the meat-eating dinosaurs was Tyrannosaurus rex (tie-RAN-uh-SOR-us REKS). He was strong and he was fierce. He tried to kill and eat every creature he met. And every creature was afraid of him. Only the horned dinosaurs like Styracosaurus would dare to fight with him. But even their horns did not help much against the terrible Tyrannosaurus.

Tyrannosaurus walked upright. His

front legs were short and weak. He never used them. But his back legs were long and strong. He would jump out at his prey. He would attack it with his teeth. He had rows and rows of sharp teeth in his huge mouth. He would tear his prey apart. He didn't need strong front legs as long as he had those awful teeth.

Rex means "king." Tyrannosaurus rex was the king of his world. But his world was coming to an end. All of the dinosaurs were dying. Flying and swimming reptiles were dying too. No one knows just why this happened. Maybe the land changed too much. Maybe the air became too cold for the reptiles. And the cold was killing the plants they ate. The dinosaurs all died. Now only the fossils of those mighty monsters are left. But a new kind of animal appeared to take the place of the giants.

17

THE SHY ONES

The new animals were mammals. They began to appear as the last of the dinosaurs were dying. They were not at all like the dinosaurs. Dinosaurs lay eggs. Most mammals have live babies. And mammals have hair to keep the heat in and the cold out. This helped keep the early mammals alive.

The early mammals were small and furry. They lived in the trees and on the ground. They ate fruits, seeds, and insects. And dinosaur eggs might have been tasty—if the mammals could find them.

Sometimes a little mammal left his home. First he would peek out through the leaves or bushes. If no one was around, he might come out. He had to be careful. The shy little mammal would have been a tasty snack for a dinosaur.

18

THE HIDDEN HORSE

The air on land was becoming warm again. There were lots of trees. Great forests covered the land. The first horses lived in these forests. They were not like the horses we see today. The first horses were no bigger than dogs! They did not have hoofs as horses do now. Each of their hind legs had three toes. Each front leg had four.

The first horses could not run fast. So they had to hide from their enemies. They hid among the many trees. They ate the leaves on the low branches. They were too short to reach anything higher.

As time passed, the small, furry horses grew taller and larger. Their eyes got bigger. So did their teeth. And so did their brains. Their many toes turned into one strong hoof. Their necks became longer. They could bend down to eat grass. All these changes were good for them. Because they were able to change, horses did not die out.

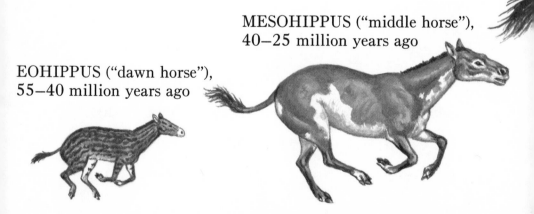

MESOHIPPUS ("middle horse"),
40–25 million years ago

EOHIPPUS ("dawn horse"),
55–40 million years ago

The world was still changing, too. Grasslands spread over parts of the earth. The horses began to live in open country. There was no place for them to hide. The only way to get away from their enemies was to run—fast! Those little horses in the woods were the "grandparents" of today's great runners.

MODERN HORSE

19

THE KILLER CAT

Lions and tigers and house cats belong to the feline family. A long-ago cousin of theirs was Smilodon (SMILE-uh-don). He was the most terrible "cat" that ever lived. He is called a sabertooth because of his two front teeth. They were long and sharp and looked like daggers.

When Smilodon attacked, he stabbed his teeth right into his victim's neck. He stabbed and stabbed until his prey died. Then he used his sharp teeth to slice up the dead body. But he couldn't chew because his teeth were too long. They stuck out and got in the way. He opened his mouth wide, and his lower jaw dropped. Then he was able to swallow whole chunks in a gulp.

Smilodon's nose was far back on his face. When he sank his teeth into an animal, the fur didn't get into his nose. Smilodon was able to breathe while he killed.

Every Smilodon died out thousands of years ago. But their relatives—lions and tigers and house cats—remain.

20

THE GREAT FREEZE

Year after year it grew colder and colder. In many places the world was covered with fields of thick white ice. These fields are called glaciers. Some of those glaciers are still there. They are all that is left of the Ice Ages. The cold was terrible then. Some animals kept moving, trying to find a warm place. Some animals grew coats of thick hair. Some learned to live in caves. Many died. But if the animals lived through the cold, they had a new enemy to fear—humankind.

21

MEET THE PEOPLE

The first people who lived on earth did not look like anybody we know. Their bodies were covered with thick hair like the animals'. But even the earliest people were smarter than animals. For one thing, they learned how to make fire. Fire kept people warm. The early people learned to make tools and weapons out of stone. They used the weapons to kill animals for food. They used the tools to skin the animals. Those skins were the first clothes.

The early people moved from place to

place together. They were safer that way.
They could defend and help each other.
The early men and women were able to
think. So they stayed alive through
the hard, cold Ice Ages.
By the end of the last Ice Age
people were wiser and stronger.
They had learned to do many
things. And they would learn
to do even more. The Age
of Humans had begun.

22

CLUMSY CREATURE

Megatherium (MEG-a-THEE-ree-um) was a giant sloth. He lived during the Ice Ages. But he did not live near snow and ice.

Megatherium was as big as an elephant. He crawled slowly on the outside edges of his feet. As he went along, he ate grass and other plants. The early people must have seen this strange monster. But he probably did not bother them. Megatherium was a gentle giant if he was left alone.

23

THE SWINGER

Glyptodon (GLIP-tuh-don) was like a giant armadillo. He had a shell like a turtle. But what a shell Glyptodon had! It was very tough and had a high hump in the middle. The shell helped to keep Glyptodon safe from his enemies. Some of his cousins even had shells on their heads.

Glyptodon had a strange tail. There was a ball of sharp spikes on the end of the tail. Glyptodon could swing his tail like a club. He could use it to attack an enemy. The early people might have met Glyptodon. If they did, they probably kept away from him—and that spiky, swinging tail.

24

THE BIG WOOLLIES

The Woolly Rhino lived during the Ice Ages. His coat of long, dark fur kept him warm in the terrible cold. The Woolly Rhino's fur kept the early people warm too. They hunted Woolly Rhinos for their thick coats and for food.

Early people also hunted other huge animals—the Woolly Mammoths (MAM-muths). Their shaggy fur made fine rugs, as well as warm clothes.

The Woolly Mammoth was a close relative of today's elephants. He had a trunk and great twisted tusks. The mammoth

had two humps. One was on his back. The other was on his head. A strange place for a hump! He stored fat in his humps. He used that fat when he couldn't find anything to eat.

In a museum in Russia there is a stuffed mammoth. He was found frozen in the ice. He had been there for thousands of years. He almost fell apart when he was taken out. But his skin was saved. He is half sitting now, just as he was when he died so long ago.

Thousands of years ago people drew pictures of mammoths. They drew them on the walls of their caves. Some of the pictures can be seen today.

It has been a very long time since anyone has seen a living mammoth. There are none left now. Once, people needed the mammoths. And they hunted them. But now all those marvelous giants are gone.

25

THE LAST OF THE GIANTS

Once, the world was full of enormous animals. Now they are gone. All the dinosaurs died. The huge mammals are no more. But the biggest animals that have ever lived—the blue whales—are still here.

A blue whale can weigh as much as 187 tons. Brachiosaurus, one of the largest of all the dinosaurs, weighed only 50 tons.

Whales ruled the sea from prehistoric

times until only a few hundred years ago. Then people began to hunt them.

Whales are easy to find. Most of the time they swim close to the top of the water. They have to dive down into the deep water for food. But they always come back to the top to breathe. As they breathe, they blow out a great stream of air and water. This shows the hunters just where the whale is.

Whales are strong and clever. They have no trouble getting away from their fish enemies. But sometimes they can't get away from human beings and their ships.

There are many kinds of whales. Some of them have "songs." The songs of the white whales sound like whistles or squeaks. Other songs sound like creaks or clicks or bangs or beeps. We hope the songs of the whales will never end. But some people are still killing whales. Unless they stop, all the whales will soon be gone. We can't let this happen to the whales. We must take care of the world's last giants . . . and all the other wonderful creatures who share the earth with us.